tredition®

www.tredition.de

AF204205

Torsten Höller

Lean and What

An essay about traps to avoid during LEAN introduction

www.tredition.de

© 2020 Torsten Höller

Verlag und Druck:
tredition GmbH, Halenreie 40-44, 22359 Hamburg

ISBN
Paperback: 978-3-347-16153-5
Hardcover: 978-3-347-16154-2
e-Book: 978-3-347-16155-9

TORSTEN HÖLLER

LEAN and *WHAT*

Reboot your LEAN Management Strategy

ABOUT THIS BOOK

First, thanks for start reading "LEAN and *What*" in that ocean of other literature.

You are interested in gaining speed in your LEAN Manufacturing Program, or you want to understand what the heck that (external) consultant they sent is doing. Or why they are doing it. Or you already know you cannot solve operational losses without manufacturing excellence. And you concluded manufacturing excellence only comes from LEAN manufacturing. Manufacturing excellence will not come from muscle work and pure exercising. Perfect, a good start!

If you delved into German translations of the word "LEAN" you would immediately stop. Here are some: "Meager", "poor", "skinny", "gaunt", "haggard", "puny", "wimpy", and the best being "slim". LEAN manufacturing or LEAN management fills the Internet and the bookshelves, while hundreds of consultants are in the market to help you with their concepts to make you "LEAN".

In 1988, John F. Krafcik defined the LEAN production system [1] or better said, gave it a name: LEAN. Obviously, he was not an expert in German language. LEAN, a system we first learned via the Toyota Production System has evolved over the decades to an overly complex field of knowledge, tools and systems that spans application from automotive to administration to even NGOs.

This book will help you to feed your curiosity about LEAN, but more importantly help you to understand the logic of the traps during such a massive change and transition, with the

---

[1] MIT Sloan Management Review, Fall 1988, Volume 30, Number 1, John F. Krafcik, The triumph of the LEAN Production System

goal of avoiding them, to be faster and more successful in your LEAN Implementation. LEAN is a big change – even you only use a small part of it. It will impact you, your people and company culture. So, if you can avoid running into similar traps that I encountered, you will be faster and more successful.

For simplicity's sake, in this book I will use LEAN as a synonym for all LEAN combinations ("LEAN and *What*"). I call it *LEAN and what* because LEAN comes with many questions and uncertainties. You can take it as a question, like "LEAN and what?" "What does it bring and what does it take!" Or: "LEAN and what is next?"

Back to implementation of LEAN. If implementation would be easy, we would not be nervous or have no large teams behind it. We are afraid: W*hat* is all that LEAN trainings and education good for if the results do not come? Or not stay! Many organizations start with energy and passion, results improve, but then you find stagnation or even roll back. You might be a leader of such a program, and you want to "roll-out/expand that program fast and effective" or you are a plant manager or director and you want to have that program "rolled out fast to eliminate my losses". You both want the same thing, but often neither gets what was expected and often misses the mark by a mile, not harnessing the full potential of what even a small LEAN Program can offer to your business and staff.

You are afraid: *What* is all preparation and effort worth if no one is using the capability? *What* if – on top of the hard day's work frustration – an extra burden associated with the LEAN Manufacturing Program crops up? Your program will slow down, resistance will go up.

Why is that? Because you ran into one of those traps. You are trapped. *How* to avoid those traps? Keep on reading...

This is what this book will help you with: avoiding traps and getting your well-designed program to your employees and business. Get rid of the losses. We will not re-design your LEAN manufacturing program. We will talk about LEAN in the next chapter but only to be on the same page. We will talk about *why* we fail, *why* we cannot change the culture or game, and *why* we do not start.

In my almost 25 years of professional work I was many times part of the implementation team for the LEAN manufacturing program of Procter & Gamble[2] in different plants. P&G has an exceptionally good – if not the best and most holistic adaption – of LEAN. Highly integrated with all manufacturing disciplines playing deep into engineering and even R&D. Many plants deliver extraordinary results – whether operational throughput, safety, quality, or speed of innovation. This would not be possible without that integrated system P&G developed based on the LEAN concepts. But even there we find different speeds of implementation and usage. Also, there you find resistance and frustration, too. I had the chance to see both great and fast adaption as well as slow implementation and pushback. But I have also seen that even after two false starts performing the third attempt right will make the difference. So, do not get hung up if the first trail was not perfect. Start all over, but this time be better prepared and avoid the traps.

The emotions I went through and the wonderful learnings I made during that time drove me to sit on the computer and write it down. Every time I could overcome some of the resistance and avoided the traps we gathered momentum, and the results improved breakthroughs and – more importantly – we quickly created workplaces where work was more fun, the value of each individual grew and the contribution of everyone was valued. When this light ignites you want to be part

---

[2] See https://us.pg.com/pg-history/

of it. You will never forget when it becomes a self-selling phenomenon. You will not forget the faces that start smiling when new problems are there to be solved instead of dragging everyone down. The power and the energy that is already in your organization becomes visible and you start moving mountains.

WHAT IS LEAN?

LEAN is an evolution that started as revolution in the automotive industry over 3 decades back. You can get green and black belts on six-sigma and try to impress someone late at the bar with them. Or at least you could try.

Many big companies have been working on LEAN for ages, some just started, and others not quite yet. You have heard from a friend that they will "do LEAN now", but "it is not working" or "it is great". You might be a fan of it, but your new boss is not. Or the other way around.

LEAN is great fun and many new words. You can make "Kaizens" (Improvements) and you reduce "Muda" (Waste) wherever you see it. You can Plan-Do-Check-Act your teams and departments or problems, improve small and big things, either in the office and on the floor. You can do "Gemba Walks" to stay slim yourself and do coaching on the floor. You will connect better with your organization. You get better focus on your customers, supply and value chain.

LEAN, however, is a complex thing. If we just look in Wikipedia and you will see almost 30 headlines that cover elements or tools from LEAN Manufacturing. And the list is most likely incomplete:

LEAN Manufacturing links[3]			
• A3 problem solving • Cellular manufacturing • Efficiency Movement • 5S (methodology) • Industrial engineering • Ishikawa diagram • Just-in-time manufacturing	• JobShopLEAN • Kanban • Key performance indicator • LEAN CFP driven • LEAN dynamics • LEAN higher education • LEAN Product development	• LEAN Six Sigma • LEAN Services • LEAN software development • LEAN thinking • Operations Management • Poka-yoke • Production flow analysis	• Push-pull strategy • Six Sigma • Spaghetti plot • Takt time • Total productive maintenance • Value stream mapping

LEAN is like the Wonderland was for Alice[4]. Many creatures that we do not understand from day one but that will have an impact to us. Can you explain why the smile is left while the Cheshire cat is gone? Maybe not. At the beginning neither do we know nor does our target group understand whether those mighty tools are friends and helpful ghosts and which of them is not. Some are simple and beneficial from day one, others need time to connect with, and some you must literally tame before you can utilize them. But over time and with some workshops, pilots, trails, training and mighty external consultancy we get clarity on the right LEAN manufacturing program for our business. I assume you did all of that and you

---

3 Overview of LEAN Terms, taken from Wikipedia article "LEAN Manufacturing", Engl. 07/2020)

4 Lewis Carroll, Alice's Adventures in Wonderland, 1865

have a program ready to launch or has been launched already. You are – technically speaking – in control of the Wonderland and able to speak with your "Jabberwocky"?

LEAN is also – and maybe more than anything else – a cultural journey. It will touch everyone. For better or worse. Be aware of that and make use of it. *Culture is not the result of the journey; it is the fuel or the brake for it.* It depends on how you use it. This book is about that kind of culture and how it will be your compass, companion, support or worst enemy if you do not avoid the traps.

This book is not a lot about LEAN Practice and Tools. I will mention a few as examples. But to learn LEAN, there are tons of literature out there that will do a better job. This here is intended to help you to effectively roll-out your program by avoiding barriers and pitfalls.

The book is divided in two parts: the first will talk about traps and barriers in a kind of technical view to them, and the second about the different roles during LEAN implementation and how they support success or cause traps to appear.

PART 1: IMPLEMENTATION BARRIERS

To better understand how we can avoid traps and implement LEAN thinking faster, it is equally – if not more –important than the question about the latest twists and turns with respect to this or that LEAN tool.

From my observations there are some traps or barriers that drive or influence the success of implementation. That collection of traps is just my experience and selection; you might have seen other ones or disagree with mine. Happy to have that discussion! Because all we do is to reduce waste in every process, doing good for the planet and our children – and at minimum, the business and people we serve.

I see barriers or traps in the following categories: No belief in success, wrong measures, internally focused or non-breakthrough measures, a broken standards system, "experts", overloaded programs, unneeded training, misuse of health checks and audits, and using LEAN tools incorrectly.

LACK OF BELIEF IN SUCCESS

LEAN gives a great box of tools and principles that empower your organization to do big things and deliver outstanding results. But any tool – even as simple as a hammer – is nothing if there is nothing to build with or believe in. You must trust that this is the only way to eliminate losses.

You have a LEAN Program already? What is your capability status? What is the leadership team's capability (about your program)? What support is obtained from upper management? What are their about it? Do they believe it will solve their problems? Do you believe it is there for loss elimination? If not, you will fail.

15

Not believing in the success of LEAN manufacturing as you designed it is the single biggest trap you can walk into. When you start(ed) working on LEAN and you went through all those books, or called all your friends that work in a company with LEAN, what were your feelings? Were you convinced? You might even read about the second revolution in the automotive industry[5]. A book that after so many years still gives the best comparison between a place with and without LEAN. But you are not in the auto industry and so you go on searching. And you find more books and trainings: Sooner or later you lose your track in that jungle. Overload and complexity will make it difficult to "sell the program" later and can cause the first wave of frustration.

Do you understand "why" you do LEAN and what the benefits are?

"LEAN" back and start believing in your program first. That belief comes from clarity on what the program delivers, and not how it works. Because the tools do work. No doubt about that.

Focus, Focus, Focus

I was once visiting one of P&G's benchmark sites, as I was working on Supply Chain those days and we had face-to-face (long before Covid-19). I was a heavy smoker back then and hence from time to time I escaped into the smoking lounge, where you meet all smokers, be it from the floor or the offices.

We made some small talk as you have in those break rooms and listened a little to what others around me talked about. And it was unbelievable what I heard. Everyone – and I do mean everyone – was

---

5 Die zweite Revolution in der Autoindustrie | Womack, James P., Jones, Daniel T., Roos, Daniel, 1992/The Machine That Changed the World: The Story of LEAN Production | Womack, James P., Jones, Daniel T., Roos, Daniel, 1990

talking about rapid changeover. A program like Single Minute Exchange of Dies (SMED) to speed up your product changes on the equipment to reduce planned downtime. Comments like: "the C-Team yesterday made in XYZ minutes" and "Wow, great!" spewed forth. Everyone was aware of the recent results and achievements. Everyone was proud and indirectly cheering those that made it.

So, I asked for the background and why it was so important to them and why the whole site was focusing on it. And I learned they recently recognized that – as a plant – the way they looked at their production losses was imperfect; not to say wrong. They always had looked at unplanned losses and never planned losses, where changeovers matter. Once realized, they saw that this was their single biggest loss on production. Consequently, their program was fully focusing (for a period) on that one thing: Change over time reduction. Everyone was "all-in" and could help, be it warehouse, supply chain, operations, planning and so forth. All were aligned and clear on the loss would be tackled together. I do not have the numbers of how fast they improved their throughput after that, but that plant still is benchmark in P&G, so I assume this was not the last topic they solved in that manner. Focus – and believing in that focus – is key.

You must believe in the value of the program and be able to explain the value and benefits. You must convince others by that belief and not via authority.

Why? Let me explain it with an example. You might made such or a similar experience already in the past:

Someone from HR that you know for a long time comes around and tells you to fill out that new form and says it is a kind of a survey[6]. So, the person comes in your office or it is mentioned during a weekly meeting, the discussion unfolding usually as follows:

*You: **Hello**! HR: Please fill this out by end of next week! You: **Why**? HR: Because it must be done! You: **Why**? HR: Because it is globally monitored, and we do not want to be in the spotlight! You: **Why**? HR: Hmm...All managers must fill it out! You as well!*
At that point you give up getting an answer to the why and because you cannot escape it either way.
*You: **How** does it work? HR: It only looks complex, but it will only take you 10–30 minutes to do, you will learn quickly once started.*

They hand out the tool and the so-called "one-pager" that is actually three, and leave telling you: "You will learn it while you go". You try it, and after five re-starts, seven reminders and twice saved to the wrong place you deliver what was requested on the very last day in the very nick of time.
But then you must make five adjustments because you filled it out imperfectly, finally submitting a perfect version with only a few days delay.

The results and outcome of that survey was that you never got any feedback, but instead learned that your plant was not reaching the 100% completion on time rate and questions from top management about that arose.

Raise your hand if your stomach just started to wince in pain even thinking about that! You ask yourself: What is

---

[6] If you work in Human Resources , think about the HSE department approaching you for that super new system they want to be used now also in the office to further reduce the risk of incidents caused by open containers of chemicals.

the value-add for the company or what was the problems we solved here?

You do not want your target audience and customer to feel like you did in this HR example when confronted with LEAN.

Let us look how that could feel for you: You, as the on-site Operational Excellence Manager or LEAN Manager, come along with your brand-new LEAN Program. It has a powerful name, for sure. Twelve months back you were picked to develop that program for the company, implementing a powerful team of experts, even employing external help.

Now you stand there in front of the crowd with a complex presentation and a big booklet (because LEAN is complex). You talk a lot, show multiple tools, and are enthusiastic about those LEAN ideas and concepts. You tell the audience it is easy, and we will "learn while doing". Everyone is impressed. And everyone's stomach is starting to grumble, as they end up feeling you do not really believe in what you say, given that you just explain what it is and how it works.

Or as the plant director or operations manager you were just listening to such a presentation. You see the LEAN program team is fully engaged – obviously, all are experts are into it. It sounds like a project at best: or is it just another form to be filled out? At a minimum, it is work. A must-be-done item. A management-told-us-to-do-it thing. And you will implement it in your plant(s) on top of the multiple crisis you have to endure every day. You roll it out, but you do not believe in it, because nobody delivered arguments for that apart from "we do lean now".

And you, as consultant, have the pressure of "rolling out" that thing quickly and want to monitor its implementation. The program is expensive, needs many resources and has senior management's attention. Failure is not an option, so you add some complex tracking over the roll-out of lean, because you do not trust the belief.

Consequently – and quite soon after the kick-off – a lot of the energy is gone. The first trap has been triggered. Our organization is not engaged.

You might now say: "Wait a minute, I fully believe in the program. It works. It was proven factually to work in that other plant, in that other company we visited, in the examples we went through, in the small pilot we made and so on. And now this author tells us, we do not believe in it?'

I am quite sure you believe in it. But we need to get that fire and that spark over to the plants and organizations. And, as with any other change, this is a challenge. But it is touching *everyone* on site, hence it is far more then introducing a new project management tool or an SAP client that is connecting with some experts. We need to get across the true objective behind that change to LEAN. Why are we doing it, what are the reasons behind it? It is not "management told us": It must be clear that LEAN is the only way to eliminate losses, gain growth for the company and get everyone fully engaged, in synch and onboard. We need to get the focus right.

So, how do we link this focus to the everyday work? With the right measures. Where the next trap is waiting for us.

MEASURE THE RIGHT THINGS, NOT WHAT YOU GET!

You have built a wonderful message for the people that outlines that with LEAN and its tools and methods that will enable them to change the status quo. The focus is there. People talk about it; they look forward to getting things moved. Here is the next trap looking for your feet to let you struggle because we tend to make it too complex – especially if we start measuring things.

These boys have a simple measure: Get the shuttlecock!

So, let us also simplify this a bit: Companies are there for a reason. They produce something others want or should buy. And they must make a profit. Profit is simple. You need to have a (far) higher sales revenue than the sum of your cost of goods and delivery. However, even if you make profit, the company with the higher profit and growth will most likely more successful over time. Hence, management must be eager to make profit and grow faster to dominate the market against the competition, on Wall Street and so on. Sure, companies nowadays have more responsibilities in and outside their walls, but in our context, making profits and growing sustainably just will be OK for now.

In manufacturing and in whole product supply, we can support those two company goals (growth and profit) in great ways. We produce what we sell. We ensure product quality. We distribute it on time in the right quantity. We do not waste any product in our inventory or throw it away because of quality defects. We are productive. We enable growth by better throughput or fast start-up of new capacities. Our costs are low. We make consumers happy because we in manufacturing and supply chain deliver the goods. Or at least we should. But reality does not always work like that.

> ### Get clarity about losses
>
> When I took over that one team, they looked at throughput in a way I was not used to. For the bottleneck equipment they looked at weekly delivery volumes only. The company wide defined efficiency number (Overall Equipment Effectiveness) for production was tracked somewhere in a scorecard but

not used as source for their loss tree. Bottlenecked equipment was already a 24/7 issue. If they did not reach the volumes one week, excuses were sent out to sales and distribution team and it was tried again the following week. Business was on allocation at that time and plant was far away from providing capacity for any growth. Unit costs were high. They did workshops on loss elimination but with limited impact to results, given that focus was on the "how" and "the number of people trained".

I took my lead-team aside and agreed with them that efficiency tracking would be taken out of the attic back into the daily routine and that we would start analyzing our losses on this basis – because whether the weekly volumes were reached or not, it did not tell anything about equipment efficiency.

They did as were told and quickly we began to have clarity on the losses and began to categorize and eliminate them. We taught ourselves, trained our people on loss elimination, on autonomous maintenance, TPM and others, and we **could explain why: growth and cost.** And as we worked on one issue followed by another, with the clarity of the loss we could measure progress: waste went down quickly, as did unplanned downtime. Thus, we **proved that the specified losses could be eliminated**. New and better standards were established. Long story short: After little more than one year we got our equipment from ranging 50% to 65% in output to above 80% and 85%. Believe me, having the right losses on track is pure adrenaline for everyone in every plant, and the best argument to utilize LEAN.

So, understand your shuttlecock and let the game start.

MEASURES ARE INTERNALLY FOCUSED AND TOO DETAILED

Too many times we are hunting *a too detailed level of measurement* in the KPI (Key Performance Indicator) system. Plants are overwhelmed with their KPIs and their performance measures. When I was student of Business Administration in Germany in the early 90s, KPI Systems were in every new book published – the more measures the better. The more complicated the KPI system tree, the cooler. And the saying was: "You get what you measure".

This is still true today: You get what you measure, and we have far more data today than 30 years back we can track and follow up on. There is technology available and implemented in many sites that controls every (!) sensor and motor, pump, end stop, filter, container, or gear on your equipment. You get data from SAP and other sources.

Be very choosey on what you measure and what measures represent the true and direct indicator for your external focus. That external focus helps you linking your LEAN program to the real world.

Many measures in your KPI (Key Performance Indicator) System have an almost obvious link, like, for instance, costs. Examples:

- Machine throughput as output/time
- Machine output as % of installed capacity
- % of waste per unit produced
- Quality defects found in the market

Every unit you do not produce is lowering productivity and increasing your unit costs. Each quality defect has impact on future sales and growth and might incur cost to change. Other measures are supporting the above ones directly, such as if you

- measure internal quality holds
- measure breakdowns of your equipment.

Breakdowns have to do with machine throughput, since equipment is down, not producing. But is only a part of the whole losses in production cost. Other losses also play into production losses, like not enough staffing, no raw materials delivered, feeding issues, full warehouses, waste, operational errors – you name it. Out of a potential 100% you might reach 85% output, meaning 15% is your total loss here. You can convert every percentage point into cash and let it speak by itself.

At that level of your loss tree, you can easily explain the links of tools and processes of LEAN for the losses. For example, tools to reduce your breakdowns will be used if breakdowns are high, if your plant absenteeism is the main cause for production shortfall you must pick others. So far, so good...

But sometimes we dig too deep, like the dwarfs in "Lord of the Rings". Let us assume breakdowns is 10% of your unplanned downtime of equipment (i.e., 1.5% of your total loss, assuming you reach 85% output).

If behind that 10% breakdown loss you found something like "meantime to repair in case of an unplanned repair" is 25% of your downtime on breakdowns. In your further analysis you see out of that 25% repair time 40% is because staff are untrained for it. So, yes you work at a loss. But let's do the math: 15% (production loss) x 10% (breakdown) x 25% (too long) x 40% (untrained staff) = 0.15% of your entire production loss is from that "people are not trained to do a repair if unplanned breakdown occurs". As a reaction, you start measuring "training". I lost you! Wonderful! This is the same that happens to your organization if you get too nitty-gritty.

If you trust that from the detailed analysis you expect everyone will see the clear connection to costs, you will be quite alone. That level of details only will be reached later when you start implementing LEAN and more and more people are involved in loss elimination. At the beginning, stay on a level with a clear, compelling link to the business needs.

Link business loss to what people want or need.

Once we worked on unplanned downtime as our loss. We wanted to get this to down to zero.

The equipment and processes were overly complex in that business unit and probability was high that one of the many thousand machine and material parameters was not perfect and stopped the production. Then the operators had to thread all materials again, set everything up for running and pressed start-button to see whether it worked. There was a high probability that it would not with the first trial. So quite some hectic moments and many minutes later the machine was up again; the operators wiped the sweat from their faces and crossed fingers that this would not happen too often during their shift. Some teams had more talent and/or luck then others, but every shift could offer surprises, and not every shift was easy. They called it "battlefield shifts" if they had multiple of those issues.

The loss for the business is obvious. You make less product and unit cost go up. But here we had a clear link between a business loss (unit cost) and a loss for every operator (stress, hectic, all unplanned, etc.).

> Once aligned, we worked together successfully towards almost zero in less than 18 months, utilizing the power of chosen LEAN methodologies.

Too many times **internal** measures become external ones. Be especially careful with measures you introduce with LEAN, such as people trained, the number of workshops held, the number of qualified trainers and so on. Those are important measures to track progress of LEAN, but not an external need. If you measure how many people filled out the form correctly, what message are you driving? Importance of paper, but not importance of external results like profit/cost or growth.

LEAN a is way and a mean – but not the ultimate target.

UNCLEAR ON BREAKTHROUGH

Assume you were smart as you are, and you do not have too many items to measure. Your level of detail is not too fine. Still there is one last item to be ensured. There must be *breakthrough* items defined. If you set up your LEAN management program for success, you should not link LEAN to the frequency the on-site cafeteria has your favorite lunch.

You had better make a list of the true (external focused) losses. In the end I am sure it will be a short list. LEAN will typically improve your numbers drastically:

- 3–8% of productivity year on year,
- double quality results,
- cost reduction of 1–5% year on year,
- and cycle time improved by 50%, etc..

Not small of any kind. None of them. But which of them is the main one? If that is clear you need to ensure it is visible and clear to others, as the rapid change over one item was for the one plant in Procter & Gamble. It does make sense to repeat this exercise in small scale every year, and more thoroughly every 2–3 years. In Procter & Gamble, this was called the compelling business need.

Both as leader and as consultant ensure you have clarity on that, and the organization understands it clearly. What does the business really need? Is this clear to everyone? Yes. If you now link this to the everyday work of the people, e.g. how does the breakthrough loss look from their perspective you get the buy in.

Translating the breakthrough message. On the journey towards eliminating unplanned downtime, we talked to all teams and operators about what it will look like once we eliminated all unplanned downtime. I – as the leader – had a clear picture of it in mind. Everything planned, every shifting like a Formula One/Indie 500 racecar, with well-defined and perfectly organized pit stops at predetermined times. No surprises anymore. You come to work, and you know what exactly will happen on your shift and who will do what. Then you go home, and it was a perfect shift.

In that context I talked with one of my most senior operators, a shift leader in his 60s, decades with the company, a very experienced and trustful person. I wanted to get his opinion and asked: "Can you imagine, do you believe that we can have only planned shifts in the future?"

Answer was: "No, I can't imagine. It will not work; machines are too complex!". I was shocked because I thought everyone would be happy to avoid "battlefield shifts". So, I asked differently: "Would you wish to have such a shift?" "Oh yes, it would be great to have it like that, no stress, no sweat, no tears", he replied, "but I can't imagine it works or will be easy".

Now we had a basis to start from.

Link those defined losses with the right tools, work processes, and principles and you will get a long term buy in from people on the floor and from management on LEAN manufacturing and you can see fast progress.

Hence, if you are not crystal clear on how your LEAN program is linked to that specific prime and breakthrough target, how can the extended leadership team in any site of the world explain the benefits to their teams on the floor? Will they just deploy the new standards? And what will those people say if they come home after the first site deployment session of that new *"we save the world"* LEAN program? You know it. They will call it "just another program they roll out". They will not understand what is in it for them. They might understand it will save costs and increase productivity, which people on the floor or in the office might translate into "I will lose my job".

That and other private talks will be the fertile soil for a very unsupportive culture against your LEAN program. Soon people will find mistakes in the booklet and things will go wrong – as they sometimes do. For your target group, all of that will be a prove that LEAN is not working and will never yield benefits while only creating effort.

With other words, you are finished at the starting line before the race even starts. But, if you solve the most burning issue, you will get the red-carpet treatment.

We must understand that LEAN is just there to eliminate losses and nothing else. This is our belief.

Your job as business leader together with your consultant is to define that connection. Explain it to everyone clearly enough. That is your true belief. Always go back and help people to manifest the link to losses. Utilize the compelling business need with some visualization (Shuttlecock!).

If people and leaders start doing "that LEAN program on top of their regular work" or in "workshop style only" you will not succeed, and LEAN will be of no help. I have seen that even at Procter & Gamble. If you notice this, you must correct it fast.

Once you are over that hurdle, the next one awaits.

BROKEN STANDARDS SYSTEM

No program comes without new standards. Correct? New standards are the official sign that something happened. Every element of your program has a standard connected with it. Execution of LEAN tools will result in new and mainly better standards. To confirm: Standards are fundamental in LEAN manufacturing. Because standards are the answer for solving a problem. If you have a problem, ask for a standard. If there was a standard and it was used, it might be not good enough. Improve the standard. If there was no standard, no wonder it did not work. Create a good one; a simple one that perfectly fits the loss.

The key is to have standards. So what is wrong with that?

Nothing. We need standards for almost all aspects in LEAN. But standards are misused, often are wrong and not executed in their true intent. This is not because of LEAN. LEAN is just tapping into this trap. Because **standards are only used when**

- **standards help people and when those**
- **standards make sense to them.**

Have you ever stood in front of a stop sign in an area where perceived 500 miles around had nothing besides you? Have you ever noticed how many signs, letters, and notes that you can find just by walking from the parking lot to your office or workspace? All needed, all up to date, all make sense? Do you like going to the authorities filling out that many paper forms to get something done, or are you a fan of finishing your tax declaration early?

All those signs, rules and paragraphs are just called a "standard" because somebody said: "This is the standard for this and that". But they are not a standard in the way we need them in LEAN manufacturing.

You will have a fast deterioration of standards if they are not good. For sure you observed something like that: Somewhere in the plant new standards were introduce and in the first days everything was tidy, and you can see the sticky tape everywhere like a lighthouse in the dark. Maybe flanked with a selection of prohibition signs.

Very soon after introduction you will find a deterioration and weakening of the standards and things become in disorder again. This deterioration is for sure a loss, but we could still smile about that. But worst is if people do not follow standards and procedures and get seriously hurt.

The picture on the right I took in 2010 in Egypt, opposite the house we lived in. I am sure it is not in line with your expectations of safety-standards.
If you work in a plant that never had an in-

cident, please let us know. Because those deviations from standards (typically less risky) happen in many plants and operations. Every day. People do not follow the standards even when these would help and protect them. That is crazy! And: Why is that?

Are they trained? Yes. Are the capable? Yes. Do they have sufficient time? Yes. Do they – or better said, do we – believe that all the many standards help or are worth the effort? No.

We all live in what I call the *standard bubble*. It is dangerous because many people (mainly leaders) feel safe since so many standards were "implemented", "deployed" and "rolled out". Or as people say, everything has a standard! So, we are surrounded by a bubble of standards. Every standards owner is postulating: "We have a standard [for that] <u>and</u> all are following it [because all are trained]".

But standards are not followed automatically just because they exist and/or people are trained in them. We all live in a standard "bubble". This bubble suggests safety to us, but it is not safe. Any small thing – like a needle – would prove that.

From my perspective, here is the **main threats to standards:**

1) Too many standards
2) Low-quality standards
3) Standards lacking intent (for the sake of... standards)
4) The standard deployed with the watering can
5) Standards not aligned
6) Standards that never die

Let us delve into the threats in more detail.

1) *Too many standards.* Production plants are large and complex. It requires a lot of standards to run them. There are legal requirements, standards how to operate the equipment, for correct storage of goods or standards to check quality and work safe. The list could be endless.

From an operator point of view, it becomes incredibly complex to have them all in mind, recognize them and finally to always follow them correctly. If there are so many standards there must be an order, a priority of standards. We can agree that safety is first, then quality and then.....? What is next on the list and why? We have too many to remember and consequently do not see the forest through the trees. Hence, everyone is having his own sequence of standards that are important to them. Less important ones have a higher probability of not being followed.

And this problem with standards already exists before you start to roll-out your super cool and new LEAN standards! It is important for you to understand how your organization or the organization you go to for LEAN implementation is inflated with standards. If they already have too many your new standards will be just one-in-a-million. This will be a problem. Because this inflation of standards is impacting the entire standards-system, making noncredible and thereby endangering your LEAN program roll-out.

But your LEAN program can – and will – help to clean the standards landscape and reduce the standards bubble (see also threat #3).

2) *Low quality standards.* You know them. You have seen them. You have received them via email. Your stomach likes them, such as "fill out that form". Everyone knows they are no good, but they exist and "have to be followed". Some so-called 5S standards are a classical example, but unfortunately also many HSE standards fall under this category. Extensive follow up is done with tours and others measures to get discipline in standards execution – even for those low-quality standards (instead of making standards of high quality). Here is the next opportunity for LEAN to help to improve *all* standards.

Low quality has some dimensions:
    a. *Too detailed.* What started as "OnePointLession" goes over several pages quickly. Nobody will ever read it. Only the originator understands everything. Nobody reads to the end.
    b. *Explained as if for a child.* Not one single person on-site is stupid. But many standards explain it like they are dealing with children and not mature people with long years' experience. If you start fooling the people, they will not follow.

    c. *Not from here.* I –as a stranger or new kid in town – would not try to explain a route to somebody in that town. But many originators of standards do. They can manage from their office even and tell people from somewhere else what to do. Instead of going in contact with the operators on the floor, they develop the route, the map, and the standard. Which typically results in low quality.

    d. *Not updated.* If a standard is requesting a red button be pressed, ensure the red button is not yet replaced by a blue one or that pressing any button will now result in damage. This has overlap with "standards never die" below.

What does a low-quality standard do to your entire standards system? It will impact it because these will be the examples used when people complain about too many faulty sets of regulations. And they will (they must) find their own way to execute that task. Build their private and personal standard. Every personal standard to one and the same topics with some deviation to next one and for sure deviating to the official but low-quality standard. The opinion of the people about standards is: All standards are erroneous, do not follow them. And they will not acknowledge the power of good and correct standards existing Example: *If you put a rotten egg in with the scrambled ones, all is lost.* Adding good ones now will not repair it. Every single standard in the system need to be of outstanding quality.

3) *Standards without intent.* This is linked to our discussion on losses. Too many times we have standards for non-existent problems. Especially written procedures and interaction with administration are full of them. LEAN will help you quickly identify those you need and those that can be eliminated. The effect of standards without intent

is as above: the whole system of standards is seen as not making sense. Sometimes the reason (the loss) is no longer existing. Regular clean-up is needed. This might not the job of the LEAN Team alone, but if there is too much of a legacy of nonsense you cannot win.

4) *Standards not aligned.* Watch out if standards are not aligned between different departments, it can happen that department(leaders) declare this standard for "not needed here" because they do not agree to the standard.

5) *Deploy with the watering can.* Somebody made a good standard. It solves a real problem, is easy to use and is of high quality. The originator can be enormously proud of that. And they are: they feel it is important that everyone on-site – including the plant manager – is trained, not only the folks with the problem. Which then leads to point no. 1, where have an inflation of standards – or from an operator's perspective, to a standard not required, as mentioned in point no. 3)

6) *Standards that never die.* Standards once established are like taxes introduced by government. The reasons for introduction of the tax might be long gone, but we still pay it. This is also true for standards: They are seldomly challenged, and if they are, the originator fights for his "baby" and as long as everyone believes there is only a need for more standards but not less (we see that inflation). Look at the many outdated notes and info letters that plaster the path from the parking lot to the office.

Based on these inherent insufficiencies in the standards system, there is an imminent process where people choose which standards they will follow and those they will not. Like you in front of the lonely stop sign in no-man's-land or the folks on the self-built scaffolding in Egypt. Sometimes that decision is OK, sometimes it will be fatally wrong.

If we know about that threats and start to bring the standards system in shape by utilizing LEAN methods we eliminate losses, we are on the right track, we have a far better chance to implement LEAN and to save money from the first minute. And we have very thankful plant population that only has those standards they truly need to work effective, efficient, and safe. And with LEAN you enable almost everyone to help creating and optimizing standards and processes. A great motivator for many.

Your role as a leader is to ensure you are role-modeling standards. Ask for standards, let people show you the standards they use, help improve the standards, or stop standards when not needed. You as a servant leader are key to demonstrating why standards are important. The lower your expectation is on standards, the higher the risk that people will not follow them. If you feel it is important that the handrails on stairs be used, then use them!

Remove the spillage

I was working in one of our biggest plants at Procter & Gamble, leading the Production Planning Department, co-located in a side wing of the exceptionally large building. Thus, I had some – but not too much – insight into what was talked about "in the plant" and whether standards were an important topic there.

However, one day I was walking down one of the endless aisles and I saw our plant manager from some distance walking alone in the same direction. She obviously found something on the ground. She stopped. Then walked away and shortly later came back with a cloth she fetched herself and removed spillage that somebody else had caused.

I cannot tell how surprised I was: She was the plant manager; she had the highest rank in the hierarchy on-site. And she was removing spillage! And she obviously did not do that because she was being observed; she did not notice me until I was closer. She just did it because standards were important to her. And this was the message I learned – and I never forgot. Still today, I cannot pass by litter or dirt.

Summary: If we just keep adding new standards into a broken system, we will be frustrated soon. There is a standard bubble with several different dimensions or threats of which we need to be aware. Understand how big it is and what are the main drivers of that (broken) system. If you roll out a new standard, do not expect it will be followed automatically. Leaders must role-model the standards.

THE EXPERT CAN BE AN OBSTACLE

We are experts in what we do. We have worked our topics for many years, and we are good in it. It is particularly important in LEAN to have or to be the expert to select the right tools, to generate the training or do workshops.

But we tend to be like a gardener who always tries to make things better then mother nature. Nobody else can recognize, see or can make use of it. We start to explain in colorful words what it is all about and the Latin names of all the flowers, bushes, and trees. How wonderful it looks in October we already explain in March, while in October we look back to the nice summer when the whatchamacallit tree was in full bloom. And we overload everyone who unluckily comes too close to us with details. Sure, we impress everyone with that knowledge and experience. But this is not what the person was looking for that came to you. They have a loss in their garden and do not know if they are doing something wrong or missing a step. They ask for a better standard or a tool to assess their current way of doing the things to adapt these standards themselves, and not to be proven stupid.

In LEAN it works similarly: we know so much and have so many items and tools we have studied and learned. Especially as a consultant – but also as experienced leader – you must be selective. Work it bit by bit. Bring everything into a logical flow. Give the people the help they want. If they are aligned to the beliefs, they admit they have losses and will start asking questions. And you will provide the correct answers to them. Specific. To the point.

DO NOT OVERLOAD THE PROGRAM

LEAN can be extraordinarily complex. Decades of science and practical experience fill the bookshelves. Our task is to simplify everything in a way that people can easily grasp it. And I am not only talking about the content of the specific tool: I am also talking about the context in which we provide it.

A lot of training and booklets are too complex. We cannot tell everyone that we should develop simplified standards based on 5S and that everything must be "Poka-Yoke", yet our training are looking as if they come from the 1960s and are overcrowded with knowledge nobody needs. How should people feel when they are confronted with that? They will deduct this from your "goodwill account"! Also ensure that the trainer is schooled as a trainer and is not dumbing down the slides that have only text on them. This is not leading to engagement. There is a lot of modern technology at hand to make good trainings and selective content. Start using it.

The same is for the booklets or other reference materials, they are too big and too heavy. They do not provide information at your fingertips. Like with standards, ensure all is up to date and not containing 20 years old pictures of equipment dismantled long ago, for instance.

The other thing I noticed over the years is that holding the training was one thing, but getting it documented correctly and ensuring we followed the book to deliver that capability was eating almost as much time as preparing the training itself. Many places have an education and training system that is a monster – even when it is packaged as modern e-learning it is tantamount to getting work done. (*See also below under support.*)

No need to re-do your LEAN program, but only to question whether it is overwhelming or placed into sufficiently small packages to be absorbed and understood (and used) by your target group? Is it really addressing the losses your organization is confronted with? Is it easy to learn? If not, people will not come to ask to get coached.

I like a lot how, in his book "LEAN-Start-up"[7], Eric Ries uses the idea of an functional sample with cycles of A-B Tests to find out what customers want. The book is intended for Start-ups, but you can do the same when you work on LEAN in your company. Prepare something for your customers, test it; if it is good, then go on. Do not prepare the entire program with too many details over a five-year horizon and try to roll it out all in one shot: Its will not work.

TRAIN ONLY ON WHAT IS NEEDED!

Once people understand that LEAN tools do eliminate losses and are empowered to use the tools, they want to learn more and more about advanced tools. Once they understand that some LEAN tools and processes keep the results up and they accept that LEAN is not a "project", you have done a good job up until here.

But do not go overboard now. Less is more.

Everyone is eager to learn something new. Some people train hard and with passion new dancing steps or how to make a somersault from a 25-meter-high cliff into the ocean. You also have a hobby, and you train hard to become better at something. Without the know-how you cannot execute your hobby.

Nobody will call work every day his hobby, but many people do have passion and energy for their work and want to become better. They recognize their deficiencies and want to be able to correct them.

But there are tools and capability that do not pay out the next day. Many systems are there to support loss detection or are there to keep results up sustainably. Or you needed to

---

[7] Eric Ries, The LEAN Startup - How Constant Innovation Creates Radically Successful Businesses, 2011

break down certain capabilities in smaller segments, and only the fifth segment (the last one) will tie everything together.

Still, you will have to train them all. Hence, it will occur that not everyone is passionate for that new process or tool from day one onwards. Why? The link to the losses is there, but not easily touchable or immediately visible. You need some trust credit from the organization, that the new tool(s), skill(s), or capability are beneficial. And here is a trap to lose the people.

Ensure that the effect and benefit become somehow visible and recognizable to everyone. And do not just mention it once at the beginning of the first training session. Find a way to have a steady drumbeat of examples and feedback. If that is not happening, the impression will be – even if it is a false impression – that the new tool is not solving any issues. Hence, trust will vanish. So, look on the tools and processes from the perspective of the one using or executing it and ask yourself when you could say: "This is a great tool!". Use the answer to that question to build your drumbeat.

You also need to balance the "obviously helpful" tools from the more complicated ones. If you have too many that need extra explaining and support or where the full benefit is not obvious you risk losing the people's trust.

Consequently, never train on something that is certainly never needed or will never solve a loss – even if it is a cool tool. If you do so, you risk – similar to standards – that people will feel all LEAN tools are not beneficial and the whole program confronts headwind.

Example: Think about the hammer. A wonderful and amazingly simple tool. Almost anyone with sufficient power and control can use it. The options you have with a hammer are incredible and innumerable. You can drive a nail to fix planks onto timber. You can use it to bring cobblestones into position (do not push too hard). Look on the Internet and you will find out things you never imagined one can do with a hammer. But you would never in life go around in any organization and train 5,000 people in that specific use of the hammer because you feel it is so important that they all need to learn it. You might call it "LEAN Hammering" and bring it up with 15 slides presentation. If not linked to a loss, it is waste of time. If nobody needs to fix a plank onto timber, why should they learn it? The same is with LEAN Manufacturing and its many tools.

AVOID MISUSE OF HEALTH CHECKS AND AUDITS

Health checks are needed to see or – better said – measure or indicate progress. Unfortunately, they can become a beast. The simplest **health check** is the result. But if the results are not forthcoming, it is difficult to understand what is wrong and why. And most important for you, whether it was caused by doing or not doing an aspect of your LEAN portfolio.

Develop your own thoughts and checklists about how you want to see progress, penetration, usage and understanding of the capabilities as well as the tools you want to use. Define what helps you to assess the specific situation you want to monitor. But avoid that the health check scorecard becomes more important than your production results. If health check results are used as a "target" you are trapped. Your real progress is to save costs, become more productive, improve quality etc.

Health checks are a smart way to control progress but are not the progress itself. The health checks will guide you to those areas of capability that organization or individuals are not yet strong on and hence losses cannot be attacked. In turn, however, you also find out where capability is strong and loses were dealt with, so you can utilize the strengths of those people better. You can use this insight also for the reward system or to show the connection between losses and tools, for example. Health checks are a proper way to understand where you are on the journey. Use them wisely.

If you have packed your LEAN program in steps or phases or want to see what level of capability a certain organization has reached. You might want to make **audits** at each step. Or you aim to arrange an "official result" by a defined audit or (self-)certification. I have seen examples of that in yearly shareholder presentations already. And it is also quite nice reward for people and organizations to see that they achieved a certain level of loss elimination and new capabilities.

But there is a risk with audits that people and organizations tend to just pass the audit and not use all their wisdom as intended: For loss elimination. Too many times audits become the ultimate state of achievement. Organizations do a lot to prepare for those audits, make dark corners shiny, making standards where there were none instead of just utilizing the power and capability that comes with LEAN. The focus is quickly on the how and you prove the auditors or yourself that "you do it correctly" by building up a Potemkin village. If you do so and the audit is seen like a business result: "We must pass this audit". But your real progress is limited. The problem is this: If you somehow manage the audit successfully, you confirm with the audit that you have certain capabilities that should lead to certain results, but those results will not come since the capability is not really implemented. This will raise questions later.

Summary: Your audits and health checks must not only prove you have capabilities but also that you solved business-relevant losses and will solve more in the future. Do not let them become business targets on their own; use them as intended.

INTENT VS. BOOK

"Use as intended" and "Use by the books" are terms I invented. On the one hand I saw that people changed a given and proven standard for a tool or process too quickly. This ate up resources and did not always lead to a better standard. On the other hand, people take things way too verbatim. Both will not help you implement LEAN thoughts.

Use by the book is important as we do not understand – like Alice – all the creatures in our new Wonderland. We should learn how to approach them. Do not try to use them differently then as told. In most cases it will not work. In LEAN, most standards are proven over decades as being able to solve certain losses. Use them as they are defined. If you should use the hammer to drive nails into planks, then use the hammer to drive nails into planks! Do not make music with it. It will not drive the nails – it will only make noise. Think about the loses and use the right tools correctly.

Use as intended means use it as intended and following the standard correctly. Example: In the LEAN program you find seven types of waste. The intent of that tool is to categorize losses fast and attack them fast so they can be whittled down to zero.

Do not start an endless "by-the-book" debate, a "but-the-guidebook-says" discussion or a "mister-teacher-I-know-something" call with the external consultant, whether the defect you found is that kind of a loss or another. Instead, you categorize quickly, make choices on eliminating those losses quickly; then every day you have one less problem. If you take too much time to follow the book by the letter you lose the intent – the very reason for the tool's existence.

We need it to work from those dimensions: "as intended" or "by the letter" and "reinvent the wheel" or follow the "proven standard". As you see, the only true beneficial situation is a intended use of a proven standard:

as intended	What is the important result?	if it makes a specific sound	The nail must completly be in the plank
by the letter	What is the exact wording?	If it make a specifc sound only	The nail must compleltly be in the plank with 3 hits only
		"use hammer to make noise"	"use hammer to drive nails"
		Reinvent the wheel	Proven standard [8]

If the standard is to drive a nail, whether you drive the nail hard and heavy in one shot or with three strokes does not change the tool, as both methods use the tool as designed ("drive nails"). Only that 3 shots are not "by the letter" it still delivers a result (might at higher cost/effort).

Do not change the standard and reinvent the wheel because you conclude that the important element of hammering is the sound you hear – despite your limited understanding. If based on a wrong understanding and end up reinventing the standard by focusing on the sound, then that standard will no longer work. Whether the people now follow that new standard by the book or intention does not matter. It will yield no meaningful output anymore. It will not solve the loss. You are just losing trust.

---

[8] created by Torsten Höller

Use as intended. In one assignment I was on my daily coaching tour. With one operator I looked at his inspection list. According to the *booklet,* this is a list that contains inspection tasks with a certain repeat rate (e.g., weekly or daily) in order to find defects. The long-term *intent* of this tool is that it will allow the operators to identify new inspection points or remove unrequired ones, while the immediate *intent* is to find defects before they cause trouble. When the tasks are done, they are marked in green (*booklet*), with the immediate *intent* to see whether something is overdue or has been overlooked, so that the next shift can catch up on the missing points. You could also mark it red (*booklet*) when you found a defect or deviation during inspection, with the *intent* of improving the content of your inspection list over time, like. eliminating inspections that do not lead to any other revelations. The form of the sheet was given as a site- wide standard template (*booklet*) with the *intent* of only having one template for the site.

On the sheet we looked at all tasks that were marked green. I asked how helpful this standard is for the operator's daily work and results. "Not at all helpful, all points are outdated, you cannot find defects with it", was the reply. So, I asked: why don't you change the points on that list?". He answered: "I was told this is the plant standard when it was first rolled out and we were instructed not to change it. So, I won't change it and keep my own track of inspections". Aha!

While it makes sense to not change the standard template, this misunderstood statement led to the wrong conclusion not to change anything anymore – not even the content. So, that standard was no longer used as *intended* but only as per the *guidebook*, marked green for nothing and thrown away at the end of the month. The operator was not alone and consequently trust in LEAN was low.

Not all we "deploy" and "train on" is understood and used as we leaders think. Ensure it is always used as intended.

Summary: Use the tools as instructed, but think about their intention (the objective, the reason for existence). This will make the use effective and efficient, while increasing acceptance.

PART 2: ORGANIZATIONAL IMPLICATIONS OF LEAN MANAGEMENT

After you managed all technical elements and traps, I want to talk about the organization as well as some stakeholders and their roles.

Many people – all people in the organization – are touched by LEAN. And this is good. We aim to reach everyone with the belief that together we can reduce or eliminate losses forever and faster. For the benefit of everyone. But with every person we touch we generate a reaction. In its sum those reactions will impact the culture – for better or worse.

In this section, we want to look at what roles people play when that LEAN change or LEAN transition happens, admitting and respecting the change and letting the culture alter the results.

THE GAIT

Before we do that, let us briefly discuss what LEAN Implementation is in terms of its impact on the organization. Where in our organization is it causing stress? Many people might say "LEAN is like shifting gears". I use a different term for that: Changing the gait.

If you look at a typical plant organization, it could look like that:

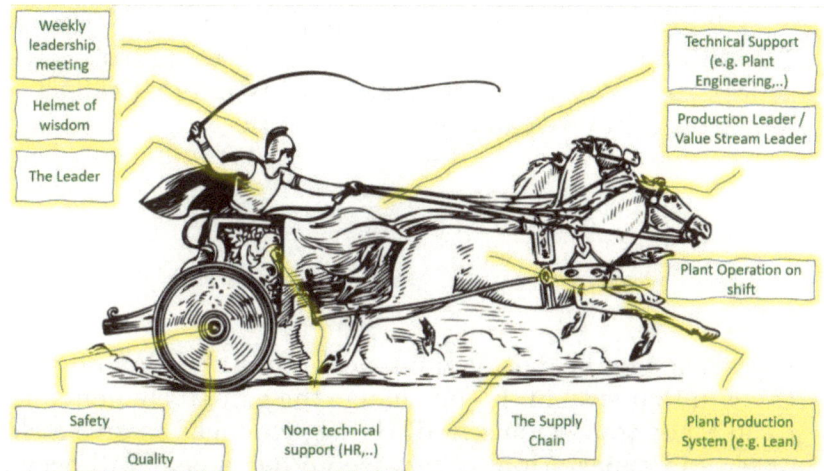

For sure, we could add more functions or design elements here. You may use different wording. Please use it (as intended) just as a starting point for exploring your manufacturing organization, your plant and what must happen when you want to change it to a LEAN manufacturer.

Most of the functions and designs will not fundamentally change with LEAN. If you have a storeroom for your equipment spare parts you will also have one in the future. May be smaller. If you have warehouse and shipping, it will stay. You will have HR and a lead team. You might add a LEAN implementation team, or you add teams (pillars) around certain capabilities or losses. But this is not the fundamental change that comes with introduction of LEAN.

The fundamental parameter you change is your **PLANT PRODUCTION SYSTEM** or Production management policy[9]. And this will come with some risk despite the benefits. And therefore, to illustrate what that means to your orgnisation, I have that change linked to the legs or hooves to imagine it as change of gait.

---

[9] MIT Sloan Management Review, Fall 1988, Volume30, Number1, John F. Krafcik, The triumph of the LEAN Production System

Gait is the way a horse moves forward. The different gaits of a horse are: Stand, walk, trot, canter, gallop, pace. We cannot say that LEAN is automatically a gallop or pace, but we can say

implementing or developing LEAN is a *change* of gait.

If you change the gait, you impact and put tension on everything in that system. If you change the gait all elements need to be ready to take on speed. Hence, you need to give a clear order and expectation, otherwise no movement will occur – and you need to ensure your system is ready to cope with the new direction.

Let me put it that way: if your chariot always stands idle, you do not need to maintain it too much. Keep it clean, remove dust from time to time. But as soon as you decide to go for a race you inspect every nut and every bolt, every connection, the wheel and its hubs, your reins and maybe also your horsewhip to ensure all are well prepared. The biggest change comes to operation and the horses.

And we do not want to see those horses like they appear to us in "Animal Farm"[10], where they work themselves to death because they believed in the original idea. Without the core – your workforce that is producing most of the added value – you will not gain speed. Which means, every single person on-site and every department and leader must acknowledge and support that change (of gait). LEAN is nothing that "they do in operations since awhile": it is a plant-wide thing.

---

10 GEORGE ORWELL: ANIMAL FARM 1945, E.G. MASS MARKET PAPERBACK – STANDARD EDITION, JANUARY 1, 1996

Read the gray box, which is why I emphasize this point.

Twisted Creed

In one of my assignment I was faced with a plant in Germany where everything, but operations seemed important. Do you remember the little pathfinder Herbie in E. Goldratt's "The Goal"?[11] In that particular plant, we in operations felt like Herbie, but there was nobody around who reduced the load of the backpack; they all put additional stuff into it and everyone wondered why we became slower and slower! What was often used as a joke internally was a big constraint when we needed to accelerate the LEAN implementation because of weak results. So, we needed to change that mindset.

Leaders of support initially did not really want to accept that change of creed. They could not understand why their super cool new standards somebody somewhere called them to roll-out ("fill out that form") was no longer the most important input to the plant masterplan and instead the LEAN elements from the P&G LEAN model were. But at least they went along with us on that journey.

Nonetheless, very soon those leaders recognized that the LEAN thinking and processes amazingly fast led to improved operational results, reduced firefighting, gave more time for improvement work, ensured fewer quality hurdles and much more. This freed up time to also work on other important standards required and

---

11 Eliyahu M. Goldratt, Jeff Cox: The Goal: A Process of Ongoing Improvement e.g. Paperback – June 1, 2014

allowed time to work losses also outside the core. This reduced stress in the support departments as well and overall site reputation grow which was good for everyone on site.

In other plants that I worked for or visited this was the opposite: the creed was that the core is the drumbeat and if the core works, they will prosper with it. So, if you enter a new plant make sure you understand whether and how much this site is "twisted".

And this is something the entire organization will have to understand and accept. If arranging training is complicated and even more so to document them, this is not the support that is needed now. The horses will bring the chariot to speed and all others must support that by making the things easier not more complex. The focus – the heartbeat – is on the floor. Like in a soccer team, everyone is important to be ready for the game, to have everything prepared, but at the end there are eleven core players that must win the game – not the coach, the medical support, the groundskeeper, but only the ones on the field. If we accept that the core is what creates speed and that the core is the one changing the gait, we have a good base to get things implemented fast but not furious.

When you start your LEAN transition every stakeholders now has a specific role to play to make it successful: They need to be aligned on the new production system and must understand that this is changing the speed (the gait) of the entire organization. All must be in it to win.

THE LEADERS

Talking about leader here is talking what the people in your organization see as the lead team. This can be the formal one with the key leaders meeting once in a week; often there is a larger group seen as the leadership on-site.

Leadership is where people look for to obtain guidance, direction, and support. You find a lot of wisdom about what the leader[12] should or no longer should be. In our context, here I saw the following characteristics as essential.

The leadership team makes LEAN successful if:
* The team is aligned and shows the true north
* They are a role model
* Every leader is an active part of LEAN progression
* They utilize the talents
* Fosters trust-> provide ownership

Alignment and true north

Sounds obvious but this is not always the case. As you have noticed in the previous chapters, core, and non-core – it must be clear what is expected will happen with LEAN and why they are doing it. There will be a strong focus on the core of production, and this must be accepted by all leaders on-site. This alignment will be reflected in your masterplan, the information you share and so on.

It is not enough to be aligned on changing the gait. Make sure that this goal is translated into a true north for every department on-site. The local leader is the best to do that and they are empowered by the alignment. True north also means staying the course if things go wrong, as they sometimes do. Maybe a training session was not perfect. This is something to improve on next time but does not signal that the entire program is faulty. Please ensure your reports and everyone you coach is clear on the fact that LEAN is the way you want

---

[12] Jim Clifton et al.: It's the Manager: Gallup finds the quality of managers and team leaders is the single biggest factor in your organization's long-term success. Hardcover – May 7, 2019

to run the plant. Our definition of breakthrough or your compelling business need statement are now of great help when you deploy the message in the extended leadership team.

Role model

Do not preach water and drink wine. Due to the massive change you initiated, people will observe you and be extremely sensitive to everything you do or not do as a leader. Example: If there is alignment and the true north expects that all leaders should spend time on the floor you must do it. If there is something new to learn, learn it. If there is a standard to follow, follow it. If the leaders are not using LEAN, not emphasizing the usage and not demand the agreed daily routines, why should the operators?

Active part

If leaders leave the implementation with the experts and are not part of the transition, it will not work. Because a big part of the implementation is done by the leaders on site, and it will also change the leader and the way the leader role is defined. If you change to LEAN as a production system you do so to lower costs, increase productivity, become faster and achieve better quality. And then you have a good reason also to change your management style or learn new ways of managing others. The leader increasingly becomes the supporter for his teams and the coach, and less and less the "Boss". I have seen many leaders being on the floor getting their hands dirty and providing support during a changeover or repair. I have done it myself. Thus, do not only come as a coach in a white dress, take your blue one with you, too.

Second to being active is also becoming an expert on LEAN – or at least in those parts that are in your direct area of responsibility. You will become coach as well and that requires you have a particularly good, almost expert knowledge in LEAN.

Depending on the complexity of the LEAN program (e.g., the Procter & Gamble one is very complex), many leader have to take over the responsibility for a part of that new capability and together with a small team develop the site capability. Over time, you become expert in many fields of capability.

Utilize all talents

It is important to utilize that huge brainpower you have on-site. Ten people gives you 80 hours of brainpower every day in an eight-hour work pattern. You can say thank you, I am the manager, I do all the brainy work. And you can make some overtime and use 12 hours of your brainpower; you are still 68 hours short every day. You add up the whole weekend 2x9 hours and finally you end up 50 hour short per day vs. using all brains on site.

And if those ten people only support with 10% of their time, this adds up to eight hours every day. This is doubling your power with just 10% of everyone. If you have 100 people in your organization, you can fly to Mars and back with that available brainpower.

But it is not only the brains but how you use them. My father once told me: While not fully contributing on work, many, many people do outstanding things after work. Go and find out. Some are great leaders or trainers; some others can make great videos or know how to run a web log or have a special technical background or are craftsmen of a special kind. When you start utilizing that talent, it will be a great motivator for engagement and contribution.

Trust and ownership

Give the people the capability and the tools to solve the problems on their own. But then do not stop. Let them use it. Let them learn and progress. Allow them to make mistakes. Do not send the experts like a fire brigade as soon as things get a little heated.

You do not want to get micromanaged, so do not do this with your people whenever they work. Trust that they understand what they are doing and why. Trust them, that they grasp the aligned goals. Reinforce where and when needed, provide data and clarity when it is missing. Coach people when they ask for help. Rewarding your people with trust when they use LEAN Tools and methodology will increase the trust in LEAN. It will show that the tools correctly used are able to solve problems, as has been proven many times.

So, if you do not interrupt when people follow the standard you gave them, this will be an extraordinarily strong message and help make LEAN a self-selling proposition. This all provides reasons for the greater ownership you want to give to everyone.

THE LEADER AS CATALYST FOR THE CHANGE OF CULTURE

I think the word culture is overstressed with slogans like "we must change the culture". As a matter of fact, you cannot change the culture. You can only change the way you set up your organization, how you operate every day, information you share, what you reward or not. You can define who has the power to make which decisions. You can bestow ownership to the shop floor. This will determine the frame for the culture. And you might go ahead and define how your future culture should look like in order to reach the aligned target and business needs.

If you need a culture of people supporting each other it helps if you can spell that out – whether you think you need a culture of risk-taking, ownership or whatever, say it clearly. But do not expect saying it will change it. Nothing will happen unless the leader start to work differently.

Because the catalyst for any cultural change is the leader and how they act. And with the implementation of LEAN elements your leaders must change – otherwise LEAN will not work.

Be a catalyst

In one of our Latin American plants someone took over a production department. She was most talented person and had a lot of passion and energy to make this department the best in the site, if not globally.

They had an overly complicated shift pattern, so it was difficult for her to reach every one of her nearly 80 people face-to-face. She was a big fan of the LEAN concept and mainly the ownership concept she saw as a key to get all shifts on the same performance. At a certain point we talked about her plans and how she was progressing. She could explain very precisely what she knew about the situation and what *she* wanted to do *personally* to change everything. I asked her whether her teams and leaders were aligned on the same issues and problems. Would they agree with the pre-defined actions? Or in other words, did she pass on any **ownership** (to build the masterplan) to the teams?

She thought about that and concluded to use a specific tool to assess the organizational capability of her team **together** with the team. Based on that output, **together** they built the masterplan and **together** delivered what was expected from them. Her team was proud of the result and she acted as the change agent or catalyst for the culture.

The the good news is: *You must not change the culture.* The culture will change when you change your production system. But you need change agents.

Your leaders are change agents and catalysts when their staff can answer these questions in the affirmative:

- Do leaders talk positive about the LEAN program?
- Do they buy into and promote it?
- Do they play an active role in coaching people on LEAN?
- Do they spend time on the floor?
- Do they follow the agreed standards?
- Do they ask for new and better standards?
- Do they give ownership to their people?
- Do they start to eliminate agreed breakthrough losses with or through their teams?

Culture is not only the result of the journey: it is the fuel, the power, or the brake to it. Use the above as a kind of health check. If individual leaders do not get to "yes" very often, then coach them.

But as soon as the people start changing in the smallest possible way, even this will start changing your culture and what is been talked in the breakrooms and smoking lounges. Do not start smoking, but those areas are a great source of understanding the current culture. Are people talking about rapid change over results from yesterday or complaining about new tools their boss asked them to use because of that LEAN program?

THE CONSULTANT

The consultant – external or internal – has only one core responsibility: The consultant is *"an expert in one or more identified areas who partners with a client to improve the client's condition"*[13]. In our context, expertise is LEAN and LEAN implementation.

Depending on the size of your factories you have, the consultant is integrated into a site position, in which the operational excellence leader or you have the role staffed regionally or globally to support the different plant LEAN teams. Or you have an external company supporting you. Does not matter too much, but ensure the following characteristics of that role can be found:

Assess	The consultant must assess the level of capability you and the organization have reached. That can be done in an audit or different form, but the assessor is the non-committed, neutral individual that tells you the truth. They must be able to support modifying your plans and focus.
Calibrate	Not only important if the consultant serves multiple plants of one company. Also, inside one factory you can find a different understanding of the diverse tools and capabilities, their usage, etc. (*See "booklet" vs "intent"*). The consultant must be able to calibrate and hence help improve the effectiveness of the implementation. They can help with examples from other places to provide clarity.

13 Alan Weis. Million Dollar Consulting: The Professional's Guide to Growing a Practice, Fifth Edition Paperback – April 27, 2016

Training	In many areas the consultant will also be trainer. For sure, they can help with workshops or specific coaching for individual leaders.
Coaching	The consultant is a partner. They must coach and support the leadership team or individuals.
Information & News	Things change. New findings need to be distributed and learnings shared. The consultant can do this during his site visits or with info letters and other similar tools, for example.
Adapt program	Again: Things change or needs change. In this case, the consultant needs to help adapt the program, so it fits better to the losses and overall business need or to the specific location.

THE COACH

Jim Clifton has a great overview of "the coach" in his book "It's the Manager". In his telling, coaching is not a stand-alone role but part of all the roles we have in every organization. So, we are all coaches.

At a certain stage during the process, technicians and operators become coaches. It is not limited to leaders – despite that at the beginning of the journey when we talk coaching on the floor, we focus on the leaders being the coaches.

Coaches bring valued customer from where they are to where they want to be.

Not sure where I learned that quote, but I still feel it is powerful to explain the role of the coach. The people we coach are VIP, very important people, valued customers of the coach. And everyone has value for the company and with our coaching, we unleash the power of them, and we help them to grow. To grow where THEY want to be and not where we want to have them.

Think back on a discussion about your favorite sports activity. You will ask for a coach to partner with you, someone to guide you to the next level. To help you to grow from within. To bring you where you want to be. But not one to tell you to do another sport.

If you want to reach something, you need a coach. The teacher in school helps you to solve problems they define. Hence, they are not a coach in that sense. Coaching is a special way of supporting others and is a skill you must ensure exists your organization.

In this old picture from ca. 1910 you see my great-great-grandfather Heinrich Noll (2nd from left). He was a coach. He brought valued customer from where they were to where they wanted to be.

As of 1913, railroad lines were established, and it was more convenient for travelers to go by train. He had stopped his business by then.

> Being a coach means respecting what people want. You cannot force them to go with you on that journey if they do not feel it adds value.

Sometimes the coaches are only staffed by existing experts. That makes sense. If people are great in, for instance, explaining how specific equipment works, then that adds value. But not always those people are the best coaches. If you are on jogging and you want to run faster, you look for a good coach – you do not seek out the fastest runner in the club.

And if you want to deal with a specific loss in your department, you go for the coach that enables you to do so. But you do not look for somebody to simply fix the issue for you. You want to be able to solve it yourself. Because this will make you autonomous. This is the great difference that LEAN will bring to your people: empower them to do more themselves. Which is a value-added for everyone.

In addition, coaching is not a classroom thing. Classroom is training. Coaching is to be where the people work or are having a problem. Give them the capability to solve their own issues and do not solve it for them. Trust them with their own thoughts and solutions.

You can picture it as being like having children. We do educate, teach, help, care for them during sickness, send them to school, etc. – but at the end of the day we want them to be independent and strong individuals when they grow up and "go their own way". We want to bring them where they want to be: We are their coaches.

Ensure you have enough people that can be coaches. Coaching is a core skill and a core role for you to change any production system to a LEAN one. Hence, ensure that leaders are trained on coaching.

THE SUPPORT

Every operational unit is complex. It has a lot of technology and/or involves a lot of people and/or systems that are needed to enable production. If you follow the value-added concept, you will agree that contributing to the product being sold and benefiting the consumer/customer is adding value. Some people work closely with production; some from more distance. Neither good nor bad.

You need somebody to ensure that the walkways from the parking lot to the building entrance are clear of snow and ice in winter. You need somebody to help you being in line with all regulations, safety, environment and health, quality, and the law. You need somebody to set up contracts and deal with the workers' council or union. You have other administrative work, and for sure there are people that safeguard that the building is – and stays – in shape. You will have larger or smaller IT or technical support, etc..

What I noticed is that those support teams tend to focus on their internal measures. They need those measures to optimize their processes. And to that extent it makes sense. But they never should lose their connection to the value-adding and the aligned plant goals or losses. If their internal goals become more important for their leaders than the throughput of the plant (or any other external business need), then there is a high risk of failure, because you lose the belief and common ground that your LEAN journey are built on.

The LEAN journey will not be limited to the core supply chain. It has tools and capability to refocus every unit on delivering added value along the whole value chain. Think back about the example of the one plant that was focusing on one measure (changeover) for a period. If in that situation not everyone is "all-in", but some support teams are still focusing on optimizing their internal measures, the overall success is endangered. Hence, support must be patient with solving their losses: first focus on the main value streams.

But in turn, it does not mean that the measures that are from a support team are not relevant as the common goal for the entire organization.

Example: In many organizations the material or supply planning organization is seen as the keepers of the inventory goals or product availability in the market. If something goes wrong "they should plan better". As a matter of fact, inventory and market availability are especially important goals for every business. Thus, the core cannot ignore and needs to work on them, given that they do so on other loses – if those are indeed "true north" losses.

Independent from whether someone is directly on the production line or plowing snow on the access road, think about respective visualization for the most important measures if that helps all your teams and in addition ensures that those measures are monitored daily and not quarterly. Again, this will be key if there is clarity on the business needs and breakthrough.

Summary: Do not distinguish too much between support and core. Use this thought as our discussion on "use by intent". Ensure that the process and the implemented LEAN capability is adding value to your supply chain and thereby your customers. Make sure everyone is clear on what the goals and "cannot miss" items are.

OWNERSHIP

Even though our factories are filled with machines and equipment to make the final product, more and more digitization and automation is implemented, new technologies are coming with IoT and so on – but people are still working there. And it is the people that still make the difference.

Some argue that "yeah, but the people on the floor must execute the work, and they cannot think about other things the whole day". That may be true for extensive and dangerous manual work. That being said, when I pack cases this does not mean my brain shuts off. I think about what I am doing and how it is being done. Where are losses and may be where are risks. I only do not have the capability and the power to convert all my thoughts into an improvement. And here is where the LEAN tools will open doors. They enable the teams to analyze and improve. They empower the teams to sustain those improvements and allow everyone to utilize the saved time to sort out the next loss, and then the one after that.

Involving everyone, engaging, respecting capabilities, utilizing talents, asking for help, allowing decision-making will change everything for your people. LEAN is predominantly changing the organization, and changing the organization means to change the role and the contribution of every single person on-site. And unused talent might be the biggest loss of all that you incur.

Manager and employees get differently interlocked the "LEANer" your organization becomes. The manager shall be less and less the "boss" increasingly more of a partner and coach. I mentioned Jim Clifton's thoughts on coach and managers already[14]. In addition, one concept that is explaining a lot about people and how we can integrate them is coming from a book that is focusing on teamwork. It is called "Do BIG things".[15]

A breakthrough team is only breaking through if everyone is in it with their hands, minds, and heart. Assuming your department – or even the whole plant – is that team. We need to get everyone on board. Nobody should sit on the bench while the game is underway.

---

[14] Jim Clifton et al.: It's the Manager: Gallup finds the quality of managers and team leaders is the single biggest factor in your organization's long-term success. Hardcover – May 7, 2019

[15] Craig W. Ross , Angela V. Paccione , et al. Do Big Things: The Simple Steps Teams Can Take to Mobilize Hearts and Minds, and Make an Epic Impact, 2017

With the typical LEAN rollouts, we address the hand and mind by explaining tools and systems. But we forget the heart. If the heart is not in it, you will not make a huge difference just by adding the capability. And it will make a difference to every individual on-site if they can be in it with their   hearts.

Example: Assuming you have a very monotonous manual job with two simple steps and high repetition rate. When you come home you do not have a lot to tell your partner or friends at the bar about the job. In this case only your hands were needed. You are good at what you do; you make everything to perfection. Nothing to learn anymore – boring!

But with introduction of LEAN you became a member of a problem-solving team and spend 15 minutes daily there (3% brainpower!), and are enabled now to lead a short daily shift briefing (five minutes; 1% brainpower) and you contribute to a better overall plan for your work team by collecting some daily data (10 minutes,; 2% brainpower). The rest of the eight hours you did your usual mechanical job – but you will remember the special items and that you now added 6% of your brain power versus 0% before LEAN. Now your mind becomes active as well and you have something to talk about in the evening. Everyone will take more and more ownership, and with that the entire organization gets more and more things moving.

It takes more to get the heart completely into it; however, we should not underestimate that already for many people a little involvement and some brain work is a great reward for them. Do not assume people do not want it.

Ownership Trap: As we see, ownership and involvement are great motors. But do not use ownership as vehicle to just move unloved work downstream. I have seen that people had to fill out parts of a scorecard for management. The data was of little value and hence went unused by management. But folks had to fill in the data every week or month, nonetheless.

It was sold under the umbrella of ownership, but it did not give them any ownership. It just gave work to someone. This is not the intent of ownership and must be avoided.

Summary: LEAN will solve your losses and will help increase your business results. And it will change all people on-site, transforming them into partners as well as contributors.

And they will give an additional boost to your LEAN journey if you let them be in it with hands, minds, and hearts.

You must believe in the benefits and the why. Look out for the traps that are there and manouver your organization around them. See how the culture will change and your results will improve.

Do not do LEAN on top of other duties. The way to improve is by LEAN. If we do not make progress, feel restasured: It is not because of LEAN, it is because you are trapped. Get yourself out there and move on.

CLOSING WORDS

Change is never easy. But if you do not change anything everything will stay the same. Do not expect better results tomorrow from a better maintenance of the status quo. Change what needs to be changed to achieve the agreed business targets. But avoid typical mistakes or underestimating the impact to the organizational environment you are working in. Do not downplay the power of the culture as a driver for change. Utilize the talents that surround you.

Allow and demand open discussion in your lead team and/or implementation team about where you are, what works and what does not, and mainly focus on the deliverables like costs, quality, productivity, safety.

But do not limit the implementation to the technologies and tools, or limit yourself to just training everyone and saying "we are 100% LEAN". This alone will not change the game.
You – as leaders, coaches and consultants – need be in it full throttle –with your heart and mind – and have the spark in your hands to ignite the fire in every organization.

What else in is *LEAN and What*? Everything!

Go out there and get LEANer every day.

Start your journey if you have yet to do so.

Your business deserves that.

Your people deserve that.

You deserve that.

Torsten

THANK YOU

Thank you so much reading. I feel it is important to have more and more organizations LEAN, so that employees become owners and results go up.

 What I wrote down here is my view on it. Maybe not everything was and is perfect. But with the coaching of James, Iris, Lothar, Michael, Bob and others, it is at least a starting point I can share helping you to avoid some traps and give you the confidence that LEAN will be a game changer for you.

I wish you the best luck on your journey. Contact me if you have comments or questions. Look at www.leanandwhat.com

Torsten Höller

APPENDIX/LITERATURE

1. Jim Clifton et al.: It's the Manager: Gallup finds the quality of managers and team leaders is the single biggest factor in your organization's long-term success. Hardcover – May 7, 2019
2. Craig W. Ross , Angela V. Paccione , et al. Do Big Things: The Simple Steps Teams Can Take to Mobilize Hearts and Minds, and Make an Epic Impact, 2017
3. Alan Weis. Million Dollar Consulting: The Professional's Guide to Growing a Practice, Fifth Edition Paperback – April 27, 2016
4. George Orwell: Animal Farm 1945, e.g. Mass Market Paperback – Standard Edition, January 1, 1996
5. Eliyahu M. Goldratt, Jeff Cox: The Goal: A Process of Ongoing Improvement e.g. Paperback – June 1, 2014
6. MIT Sloan Management Review, Fall 1988, Volume30, Number1, John F. Krafcik, The triumph of the LEAN Production System
7. Chariot Picture: https://pixabay.com/users/OpenClipart-Vectors-30363/?utm_source=link-attribution&utm_medium=referral&utm_campaign=image&utm_content=2027200 With additional notes added by Torsten Höller
8. Other pictures and graphs: private, Torsten Höller

Zeitfracht Medien GmbH
Ferdinand-Jühlke-Straße 7
99095 Erfurt, Deutschland
produktsicherheit@kolibri360.de